Merriam's Guide to Naming

SECOND EDITION

Merriam's Guide to Naming

by
Lisa Downey Merriam

SECOND EDITION

- Simple, concise, step-by-step instructions
- Real-world examples and advice
- Methodology of top branding agencies
- Works for entrepreneurs and scales up for multi-nationals
- Now includes name finding tools and resources

Merriam's Guide to Naming

www.MerriamsNaming.com

Copyright © 2013 by Lisa Merriam

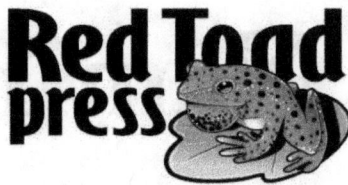

Red Toad press

Published by Red Toad Press
New York, NY 10025
www.RedToadPress.com

ISBN-13: 978-0-982082935

10 9 8 7 6 5 4 3

Dedicated to my dear friend Lauren Elkin who is quite the contortionist: Simultaneously giving me a hand up while kicking me in the butt.

Table of Contents

Preface

In the half dozen years since I first wrote *Merriam's Guide to Naming,* I've led more than a hundred company and product naming projects for Fortune 500 multinationals, mid-size companies and start-ups. As part of this work, I've helped executives wrestle with questions and deal with challenges that were not adequately covered in the first edition.

And, in reviewing dozens of magazine articles I've written and media interviews I've given, I realized I had a large body of new naming knowledge. *Merriam's Guide to Naming* was quite overdue for a redo.

This new edition is nearly a third longer than the original. The Second Edition of *Merriam's Guide to Naming* includes:
- Expanded examples and illustrations
- Updated advice for naming challenges new and old
- Name creation and discovery resources
- Guidance for contemplating a name change

Creating a brand name remains one of the most difficult first steps in creating a brand. With this expanded guide in hand, you can get past the frustration, cut time and expense, avoid common mistakes, and find a winning name.

Chapter One
The Role of Name in Branding

Your name stands at the center of all marketing activities. It is the most durable, unchanging element of your product, service or company. Because the name is the first part of creating your brand, people often make the mistake of thinking the name is the most important part of the brand. Read the Web sites of naming consultants, and you can come away with the idea that naming is the most important thing you do in branding and that it is difficult and expensive. Then the pressure is on to get a perfect name.

Naming is not ALL THAT Critical

First relax. A good name is important, but it is not *the* most important element of your brand. You might think it is funny to start a book on choosing a brand name by saying names are not so critical. But the fact is that you don't need a "perfect" name to start a successful brand.

If you look at the history of some of the world's best names (you can read some examples in Chapter Four), you won't see many created by expensive naming consultants. In fact, you can find hundreds of examples of companies with mediocre names (like Cisco) and really bad ones (like Putzmeister or eBay), that nonetheless became highly effective brands.

Many great companies found inspiration for their names in surprising places. You might think that if you need to name a sports shoe company, you would search for a name that emphasizes performance, athletic achievement, strength and power, but one global powerhouse brand is simply a play on the founder's nickname (see page 36).

Some people advise picking your own first or last name, your street address name or some other random choice—just to get started. While you can and should do better than that, don't get so hung up on the elusive perfect name that you never get off the ground. Good enough is quite often good enough. Even a bad name can, with luck and smart marketing, become a great brand.

Making a Bad Name Great

Consider the story of American Family Life Assurance Company of Columbus, Georgia. The name is too long, complex, descriptive and completely and totally unmemorable. Shortening it to the initials, a cardinal sin in branding, didn't help. You can imagine someone saying, "AFLAC—that sounds like a duck quacking."

And that is the genius. Connecting a quacking duck with selling supplemental life and health insurance isn't the most obvious idea in the world, but it worked. AFLAC is a perfectly horrible name that has become a smashing success as a brand through a witty, well-executed advertising campaign. In 2004, the company made the duck an integral part of its logo.[1] That this approach worked for AFLAC is due to the special opportunity in that strange name. And it owes much to the company's deep pockets. The story of the AFLAC name is both a cautionary tale and a success story.

Your Name Is Part of a Larger Whole

Your name is just one element of your brand. The logo, typography, and graphic designs you use in your communications, the taglines and copy in your materials, your ads, your events, your sales network, and on and on—these all work together to create your brand.

Don't make the mistake of putting too much on the name itself. We once had a client that wanted a name that meant "synthetic oil", "wear protection", and "smooth operation". It had to work in dozens of languages and have no more than 8 letters. There is no combination of 8 letters in any alphabet that can deliver on those expectations! This client was simply putting too much on the shoulders of the name. Your name is a critical piece of your brand, but it cannot, by itself, *be* your brand. What seems like a mediocre name isn't going to sink your business and, just like AFLAC, a bad name can be made into a great brand if you work with it.

Naming IS Hard

That said, naming isn't easy. On the opposite end of the spectrum from expensive naming consultants is the idea that a couple of people with a couple of beers can brainstorm a great name. Lightning can and does strike where it is needed from time to time, but holding naming contests and brainstorming over beers usually doesn't work. Dr. E.L. Kersten, a former professor of organizational communications and the founder of Despair, Inc., producer of satirical "demotivator" posters and souvenirs, rightly observes, "When people are free to do as they please, they usually imitate each other."[2] Random brainstorming without any process or knowledge of what does or does not work usually nets you a bunch of bad ideas and names that a hundred people already discovered. Your chances of getting an outstanding name from an arbitrary process is close to nil.

If you have the budget to get professional naming help, you can save yourself considerable work and risk. If you are running a big company with a lot riding on your choice, hiring a pro makes sense. But if you haven't got a big budget, you can still get a great name.

And that is the reason for this book. Naming is important, but it does not have to be a complex, make-or-break $100,000, multi-month task. The following chapters will give you a sturdy process that can work for a penniless start-up as well as for a major corporation. We provide some creative tools and practical advice to get you over the usual stumbling blocks. With a little effort, you can find and implement a name that will be a successful foundation for a world-class brand.

Chapter Two
Naming Criteria:
What Makes a Good Name

If you conduct an Internet search on how to go about naming, you'll get the endlessly repeated trite and vague advice: make your name short, easy to spell, and memorable. If you attempt to follow this advice, you may miss some of the best possible brand name ideas. Many truly excellent names are not short. Some of the world's top brands are hard to spell. And few people can tell you what name concepts are more memorable than others. I suggest you chuck the superficial advice and consider more practical criteria.

Skip the Usual Advice

Forget about a short name. Short names are often more forgettable than long ones. You are better off naming your restaurant "Fuddrucker's" than "Joe's." "Chevrolet" is a better name than "Geo." "Hidden Valley Ranch" is a full three words and five syllables of memorability! And realize: You will have a hard time getting a clear dot-com domain if you limit yourself to just short names.

Forget about spellability, too. What makes a name spellable? You can't really judge spellability unless you test a name. What looks like a simple word might not be easy to spell in practice. Some brands have actually played up their unusual spellings—John M. Smythe played on spelling vs. pronunciation in their ads for years. Do not get hung up on this issue. Even names with spelling problems can still work. Procter & Gamble is frequently Proctor & Gamble. Tommy Hilfiger is often Tommy Hilfinger. How often do people add a "u" after the "q" in Qantas? Yet, all three are strong brands.

Procter & Gamble

vs.

Proctor & Gamble

A name that is hard to spell might turn out to be more memorable. In a sea of rugged place names like Patagonia and The North Face, Arc'teryx stands out.

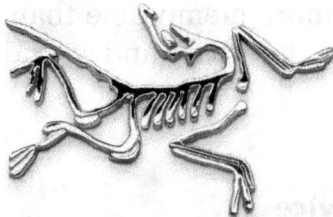

ARC'TERYX

Memorability is a tricky combination of many factors. You can't just look at a name and decide it is memorable or not memorable. Many people have rejected perfectly good names out of hand because they didn't think they were memorable. When asked why, those people just shrug. They can't articulate any criteria for judging.

Memorability is created over time and is influenced by many factors. The logo, the product itself, the advertising, the experience, and how effectively and frequently the marketing message hits home—they all work together to make a brand name memorable. The name is part of the larger brand experience, which is built over time through repetition in numerous contexts. Your brand name never stands alone. True memorability is only detectable by comparative and in-context testing over years—something you can't do when you are starting out and picking a name.

Still, memorability is important! Since you cannot just know a name idea is memorable, how can you make a choice? If the standard advice is of little use, what exactly are the more useful considerations for picking a good brand name?

Six Signs of a Strong Name
Pursuing the following six qualities will give you name ideas with the potential to be memorable:

1. Look for the unusual
"Auction Web" probably felt safer than something off the wall like "eBay", but which name is the global power-house today? EBay executives rejected a bland descriptive name for something more unusual—and that made all the difference.

The now-familiar name Google seemed outlandish when compared to descriptive names in the competitive space like InfoSeek, Webcrawler, and All the Web.

With electronic giants like Sony, Panasonic and Emerson to compete with, Skullcandy found an unusual name that helped it stand out and get a second look.

If a name idea feels risky, give it serious consideration. Surprising is always better than ordinary.

2. Be distinctive

Your name should not only be unusual, but unique.

Resist the temptation to copy someone else's good idea. Don't think of bird noises for names if you are trying to name a social media application. There is only one Twitter. Don't consider small fruits if you are naming a new hand-held computing device. BlackBerry has already done it.

Be wary of trends like the recent "fish" trend that has given us Razorfish, Babelfish, Cyberfish, even, Expirefish (they seem to have gone out of business), or the never-going-to-die "planet" trend of Planet Hollywood, Animal Planet and Lonely Planet.

Stay away from category clichés. A telecommunications company should avoid all ideas with either "tele" or "com" in the name. Words like "tech" or "solutions" are so overused they are meaningless. Looking for a name that is similar to one that already exists defeats the purpose of branding.

3. Look for meaning

Meaningful names are memorable names. But don't mistake meaning for defining. Your brand name is no more a definition of your product or business than your own name defines you as a person. Descriptions are better suited for taglines or ad copy.

The actual meaning of a word has little to do with perceived meaning. Few people will crack open a dictionary to find the ancient Greek origins or Romanian root of your name. Instead, they will look at a word and make instant associations and interpretations. Word meaning for branding purposes is determined by:
- Social context
- Physical context (words, images, graphics around it)
- Prior knowledge and experiences
- Phonology (perceived meaning of sounds)

Before Amazon was Amazon, Jeff Bezos considered the name "Cadabra" from "Abracadabra." He wanted to convey "magic." The problem was the name sounded like "cadaver." [1] Cadabra was quickly abandoned.

On a recent project to name a shopping app, the word "katagora" was a top contender. It combined "agora," a Greek word for "gathering spot" or "marketplace" with "kata," a Greek preposition for "according to." The dictionary meaning was perfect--perfect except for the fact that most customers associated "katagora" with "kangaroo!" That is why testing is so important. More on that in Chapter Eight.

A meaningful name is one that generates relevant associations and connotations. Descriptive names limit your business. Amazon is a better name than Books.com. Oracle is a strong name for predictive business software—far better than bland Computer Associates, or worse, their new acronym name of CA. That is why Starbucks works as a brand, but has nothing specifically to do with coffee.

Don't limit your brand or your business. Look for meaningful evocations, not descriptions or definitions.

4. Look for vivid names that connect emotionally

Though they are nonsense words, Häagen and Dazs evoke imagery of rich European ice cream. Smuckers sounds lip-smacking good. Outback Steakhouse makes you think of the wilds of Australia. Stonyfield Farm paints a picture of cows in green pastures. The more your name appeals to the senses, the more effective it will be.

5. It has got to be ownable

Owning your name means two things in today's world. First, you must be able to own the trademark on the word. If you are local company, owning a trademark may not seem like an important consideration, but you may decide at some future date to expand. Owning a national trademark makes that an easier transition for your brand. Even if you think you may never expand out of your local region, it pays to protect your name. If a large company comes into your market, they may be able to swipe your name out from under you.

Trademarks are awarded by the U.S. Patent & Trademark Office by class of trade. You cannot own a word exclusively and universally; only for the specific products and services you offer. That is why many well-known brands share names.

Domino's Pizza is a trademark in a different class of trade than Domino Sugar.

The word "dove" is trademarked as both a soap and a chocolate.

Long before it became a much admired electronics brand, Apple was the Beatle's iconic music brand.

As much as you might like the word Delta, it is probably a bad choice for your name. The U.S. Patent & Trademark Office already has some two thousand variations of trademarks on this word.[2]

Owning your brand name also, in many cases, means owning the dot-com domain. Nearly every word in the English language (and a good part of the Latin dictionary, too) has already been registered as a dot-com, either by a legitimate company or a squatter. Buying a name from a squatter can cost a few hundred dollars or hundreds of thousands of dollars. And there are collectors of dot-com domains that won't sell for any price. We found a winning name for a Fortune 500 company that appeared for sale by the squatter who owned it. After much fruitless negotiation, it became evident the owner just didn't want to sell. Turns out, collecting domain names was his hobby.

Owning a dot-com domain isn't just about the URL. It impacts where your brand will rank on search engines. Google "delta" and you will have to dig past dozens of pages of Delta Tools, Delta Faucet, Delta Dental, and Delta Airlines before your brand of floor wax will show up on a search engine results page.

Domain name availability and searchability are the biggest challenges to finding a good name today.

6. No acronyms--EVER!
At the risk of sounding like Mommy Dearest, acronyms and initials should be avoided as much, if not more, than wire hangers. For every IBM or BMW, there are gazillions of ITGs, ISIs, and AMAs and on and on in an endless alphabet soup.

If your name is so long that you have to use an acronym, or so off-brand that you have to hide your original name (International Business Machines doesn't sell business machines these days and Kentucky Fried Chicken does not want to be associated with fried food), then change your name. Initials rarely become a brand without decades of spending millions of dollars. If you can't make that investment, don't pick this kind of name.

Naming a brand is becoming an increasingly difficult endeavor. Getting a name you can trademark and a domain name you can own limits your choices. The time and money it takes to build meaning and reputation is on the increase in a time-starved world of many competing messages. By considering the six signs of a good name, you might not end up with your original name choice, but you will start your brand off with a strong name.

Chapter Three
Domain Name Hang-Ups
and Watch-Outs

In the last ten years, the imperatives of domain name ownership and online search have added complexity and confusion to the already difficult task of finding a good name. Because naming consultants are rarely search experts (and search experts don't understand brand names), you can get conflicting advice and counterproductive suggestions. Here is a round-up of the issues, trade-offs and considerations you need to understand.

Make Sure Your Brand Name is Searchable

Making sure your customers can find you on the Web is important to many businesses. If people enter your name into search engines like Google, Bing, Yahoo, Baidu and the rest, you want to make sure your Web page appears at the top of the search results—or at least on the first page. If not, reconsider your name. Even giant Fortune 500 companies can get it wrong.

When Computer Associates shortened their name to simply "CA," they made their brand unsearchable. Type CA into a search engine, and you will get thousands of listings for California, Canada and dozens of other entities called "CA," To make it to the top of search results, CA has to pay for a sponsored spot.

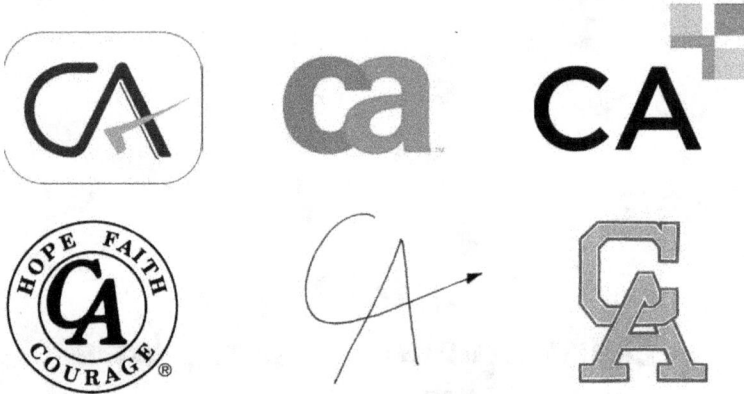

Competitors like McAfee, Novell, Oracle, and Sybase have more distinctive names that naturally show up at or near the top on search engines.

Common words might seem inspired when used in an unusual way, such as naming a hydrotherapy day spa "Water." The problem is that when customers search on the brand name "water," they end up with dozens of sites about liquid H2O before they find your day spa site.

Search Is *One* Consideration, But Not the *Only* Consideration

Search experts implore you to choose descriptive domain names that include important search terms. While owning search terms as domain names builds Web traffic, it does not mean you should use those words to name your company. Whatever their value for search, generic descriptive names can never be brands. And domains such as books.com, toys.com or drugstore.com, can be prohibitively expensive. A URL like www.WaterSpa is not only a better name for search, it is a cheaper URL.

If you are in the biofuels business, go ahead and buy BioFuels.com. But buy it *in addition* to your actual brand name. Barnes & Noble owns www.books.com and Toys "R" Us owns www.toys.com. Those generic domain names bring extra traffic and optimize search, but the generic domains are not where the companies are investing in building brand.

The story of Drugstore.com illustrates the limitation of using a generic name as the brand name. The Drugstore. com folks, despite a decade of operation, still are not profitable[1,2] and still can't break into the top twenty retail drugstore brands.[3]

Walgreens	drugstore.com the uncommon drugstore
Sales: $63,335 million	Sales: $367 million
Growth: ↑ 7.3%	Growth: ↓ 17.8%
Profit: $2,006 million	Profit: -8.3 million
Source: 2009 Morningstar, Inc. Financial Data	Source: 2009 Morningstar, Inc. Financial Data

A Domain Name Might Not Matter

People can get entirely too hung up on having a clear dot-com domain for their brand name. They reject inspired and brilliant ideas because someone is squatting on or using the domain name they want. Having a clear domain name is critical for some companies. For others, it is a nice-to-have, not a need-to-have.

If the Internet is not your primary means of sales and if your site is more of an informational site or glorified brochure, you might consider the trade-off. Is it better to have a great brand name and a mediocre domain name? Or is it critical to have a domain name, even if it means having a mediocre brand name? It is a trade-off that needs careful consideration.

Some top selling brands do not own their domain names:

PEPPERIDGE FARM
Goldfish BAKED SNACK CRACKERS — Does not own www.Goldfish.com

Canon EOS **VW** **Eos** — Neither owns www.Eos.com

HOBART — Does not own www.Hobart.com

Obviously, owning your brand name as a domain name is the ideal. But if you are looking for a short, evocative memorable name, your chances of getting the dot-com domain are very slim. Big companies can afford to pay hundreds of thousands and even millions of dollars to buy brand domains. If you are just starting out, you'll almost surely have to compromise.

Some compromises are better than others. If you can't get your domain name, try to pair the name with some kind of relevant descriptor. People will think about your brand name and your product. That is why Delta Faucet using www.DeltaFaucet.com is a fine compromise for a company that can never hope to buy www.Delta.com from Delta Airlines.

A less effective compromise is how another Delta bought www.DeltaCorp.com and a completely different Delta ended up with www.Delta-Corp.com. Neither domain is distinctive. The average person would not remember the difference between these two companies and their domain names. There is nothing to distinguish those two Deltas from the other nineteen hundred Deltas operating businesses today.

You have additional choices if you already own a company name and are naming a product. You are freer to choose the best name for your product and connect it with your company name in some way, as Pepperidge Farm has done with its site for Goldfish:

www.pfgoldfish.com

Or you can create a special section of your Web site for the product, as Volkswagen did for Eos:

http://www.vw.com/eos

What Does Your Domain Name Look Like?

Before we leave the topic of domain names, pay attention to how your name looks. Perfectly nice sounding brand names can morph in unintended ways as domain names. Some more famous examples include Therapist Finder, which becomes TheRapistFinder.com. The travel site Choose Spain can be read as ChoosesPain.com. The Via Grafix Web site ViagraFix.com seems to be selling male performance enhancing drugs.

It's not just unintended anagrams that can get you in trouble. Old economy names may be tough to spell as domain names. The name AAA Envelopes might have worked well in the days when being the first listing in the yellow pages mattered. Today, that name just makes for a bad and hard to spell domain name: www.aaaenvelopes.com.

The importance of considering domain names when naming your company or product has made naming a dramatically more difficult exercise. Yet, with an understanding of the trade-offs and opportunities, your great name is still out there and available. You'll just have to work harder and possibly pay a little more to get it.

Chapter Four
Ideas to Consider:
Types of Successful Names

Now that you have a good idea of what makes for a good name, it is time to look at types of names that companies successfully use. Looking at what has worked for others can be a great way to spur your own creativity. Before diving into your Latin dictionary, use these examples to widen the variety of ideas you put into consideration. Be aware that these categories are not mutually exclusive.

Acronym
While an extremely common choice, don't go the route of using initials for your name unless you have tons of money to spend and are willing to wait decades to build awareness for your brand. Examples of acronym names include: AARP, BP, AFLAC, IBM, KFC, TCBY, TIAA-CREF, UPS, and USAA. CVS has taken a slightly different route than name initials, going with the initials of their value proposition. CVS means Convenience, Value and Service.[1] But don't confuse that company with QVC, which stands for Quality, Value and

Convenience.[2] T.G.I. Friday is for Thank God It's Friday.[3] Sun Microsystems, the acronym of Stanford University Networks, is one of the more successful examples of an acronym name because it has a relevant second meaning.[4]

Amalgam

A number of well-known brand names come from taking parts of different words and putting them together to create something new. Nabisco is short for National Biscuit Company.[5] 7-Eleven was named for the extended hours of the store from 7:00 in the morning until 11:00 at night.[6] V-8 contains the juice of eight different vegetables.[7] Qantas is short for Queensland & Northern Territories Aerial Service.[8] DoCoMo works as both an amalgam and a foreign name. The name is an abbreviation of the phrase Do Communications Over the Mobile Network, and is also a play on "dokomo," meaning "everywhere" in Japanese.[9] Other examples are: Panasonic, MTV, Raychem, Microsoft, Duracell, Comcast, NutraSweet, Amtrak and FedEx. Be careful—some things just aren't meant to go together. Russia's Gazprom joint venture with Nigeria has unfortunately joined "Nig" for "Nigeria" with "Gaz" from "Gazprom" to form "Niggaz."[10]

Descriptive/Composition

Names can be created by combining words to describe a product, benefit or function. Bed, Bath & Beyond describes the retailer's product mix. Whole Foods sells natural and organic foods. Other examples are PowerBook, PageMaker, Airbus, Goo Gone, Toys R Us, E*Trade, General Motors and Home Depot. Watch that your descriptive name does not become too generic. Books-A-Million will never rival Amazon. And Just Hands & Feet was a great name when this company was a nail salon. They added tanning and now have the ungainly name of Just Hands & Feet + Tanning.

AIRBUS

Alliteration and Rhyme

Names that use rhyme or alliteration make for strong consumer brands. These names are fun to say and they stick in your mind, making them particularly memorable. Lean Cuisine works especially well because it combines meaning with rhyme. Other examples include: Dunkin' Donuts, Jamba Juice, Lelli Kelly, Nutter Butter, YouTube, Reese's Pieces, Roto Rooter, Planters Peanuts, Piggly Wiggly, and Brooks Brothers.

Jamba Juice

Appropriation

This approach takes an idea for one thing and applies it to another. Caterpillar got its name when a photographer said the tractor looked like a creeping caterpillar.[11] Apple is Steve Job's favorite fruit, and connotes something simple and friendly, not cold (like rival IBM).[12] Reebok is named for the speed and agility of a type of African antelope.[13] Other examples include: Java (software), Palm (a PDA), Mongoose (bicycles), Visa (credit cards), Adobe (software), Shell (petroleum) and BlackBerry (smart phones).

Evocative

Using a word that evokes a vivid image or meaning has been the inspiration of some of the best-known brands. Amazon is named after the world's most voluminous river, applied to a site with voluminous inventory and voluminous sales.[14] London Fog is named for the famous dank weather for which the coats are designed. Hooters makes a promise of more than just beer and fried food. Aloha is an airline that treats its passengers to the welcoming friendliness of Hawaii. Other examples include Eureka, Total, Navigator, Crest, KitchenAid, Frigidaire, and In-N-Out Burgers.

Neologism

Many companies use completely made up words that nonetheless convey some kind of meaning. Altoids suggests a medicinal benefit.[15] Other examples include: Wii, Lexus, Accenture, Kodak, Xerox, Benecol, Verizon and most drug names.

Foreign Word

The adoption of foreign words is a common approach to naming. Bridgestone is a translation of the Japanese phrase that means "bridge of stone."[16] Canon is the Japanese name of the Buddhist bodhissatva (enlightened being) of mercy "Kannon."[17] Volvo is Latin for "I roll."[18] Volkswagen is German for "people's car."[19] Samsung is Korean for "three stars."[20] Not every name can travel. Smeg is a venerable Italian brand of home appliances, but to American consumers, it is not so palatable. Other examples include: Pentium and Quattro.

Founders

People often overlook this excellent option. Unless you are "Smith", chances are good you can use your own name. If you can't think of anything else, your own name can be surprisingly effective. And even a common name like Smith can work in combination with another name as in Binney & Smith, Smith Barney or Smith & Hawken. The car manufacturer founder Toyoda discovered his name was hard to spell and changed it to Toyota.[21] Other great founder name brands include: Hewlett-Packard, Hilton, Disney, Ford, Dell, Applebee's and Bic (after Marcel Bich dropped the H to clarify pronunciation).[22] Of course, you will want to stay out of trouble (and prison) to avoid tainting your brand like Steve Madden and Martha Stewart have.

Nickname

If you don't like your given name, nicknames are another option. Harpo is Oprah written backwards. Danone is the pet name of the founder's first son Daniel—Dan + One.[23] Napster, Kinkos, and Adidas (named after Adolf "Adi" Dassler)[24] are other well-known examples. Product nicknames work, too. Bally is named after Lion Manufacturing's popular pinball machine: Ballyhoo.[25] And Coke is short for Coca-Cola.

Initials

Initials can be just as tricky as acronyms. Successful examples include the enunciation of the sound of R.B. for Raffel Brothers in the name Arby's,[26] (though legend also claims the name comes from the initials for "American Roast Beef

Yes Sir"). M&Ms are named after partners Forrest Mars and Bruce Murrie (the son of the president of Hershey's).[27]

Ingredients

The raw materials that go into your product may be an interesting concept to explore. Coca-Cola is named for the original formula ingredients of coca leaves and kola nuts.[28] Rival Pepsi is named for the digestive enzyme pepsin.[29] Snapple is named after its first flavor Spice N' Apple.[30] The original formula for Grape Nuts used grape sugar as an ingredient and the product has a nutty taste.[31] Clorox comes from the words "chlorine" and "sodium hydroxide", which combine to form the active ingredient.[32]

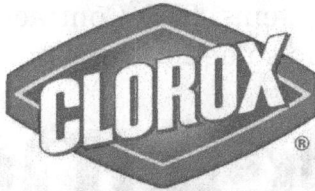

Geography

Many brand names are inspired by geography. Budweiser is named for the famous Bohemian town in the Pilsen region now known as Budějovice.[33] Marlboro is named after a posh street in London.[34] Cisco is a nickname of San Francisco (an alternative legend claims it was named for the Stanford Department of Computer Information Services).[35] Fuji Film is named for the highest mountain in Japan. Even local features can be sources of inspiration. We named an organic berry farm after a prominent dead tree that has become a landmark on the property: Ghost Tree Farms. Other examples include: Winnebago, Silicon Valley Bank, Mutual of Omaha, and Ticonderoga.

FUJIFILM

Humor and Slang

Names that make you smile can create a brand with personality, like Cracker Jack, Yahoo!, Bullfrog, and Lettuce Entertain You Restaurants. Other names can give you street cred like Skechers, which comes from the skate board culture. We named a men's underwear brand "Gladstones." A funny name is not appropriate for all kinds of businesses. For instance, you might not want to name a heart valve company something funny. And watch out that you do not pick a name that is nintentionally funny. Names like Yuki Sushi, BJ Services, Boring Business Systems, STD Contractors or WTF Group sometimes work and sometimes don't.

boring
business systems

Merged

When companies merge, they often use both heritage brands, such as Time Warner, JPMorgan Chase, Packard-Bell, Rolls Royce, and ExxonMobil. The idea is to retain the equity of each of the merging brands. The result is often less than ideal. Such names tend to be a mouthful like

PriceWaterhouseCoopers (which changed to the ill-advised, much derided, and short-lived "Mondays" before reverting to their long combined name).[36]

PRICEWATERHOUSECOOPERS ℞

Mimetics

Some companies use alternative spellings of common sounds to create unique names. Some trendy brands like 2 (x) ist, and Uniqlo have given this name style a fashion edge. Most of these names come across as a bit cheesy and retro like TastyKake, Krispy Kreme, Dunkin Donuts, Krazy Glue, Kwik Kopy, Fantastik or Kleenex.

UNI QLO

Personification

Whether based on myth, fiction or sprung from the minds of an advertising agency, personifications make powerful names. Ancient mythology has given us Oracle, Hermes, Midas Mufflers, Mercury, and Nike. King Arthur Flour uses Camelot imagery. Starbucks is a character from Moby Dick. Peter Pan Peanut Butter draws from a fairy tale. Then there are the created characters of Betty Crocker, Uncle Ben, and The Green Giant.

Green Giant™

Onomatopoeia

Using a sound associated with the function of a product is another source of brand ideas. Twitter suggests birds of a feather flocking together and chirping with each other. Sizzler Steakhouse suggests the sound of a delicious hot juicy steak coming your way. Meow Mix and ZapMail are other examples.

Clever Statements

As single word names become harder and harder to come by as dot-coms, companies are increasingly looking at clever statements as brands. Seven for All Mankind, Forever 21, and What Comes Around Goes Around are names in this style. Though lately trendy, these kinds of names aren't really new. I Can't Believe It's Not Butter has been around for decades.

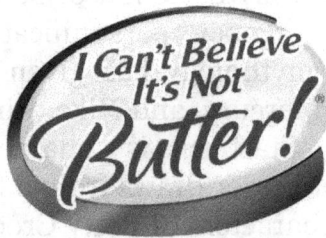

Be courageous when exploring name ideas. As you start your creative process, try coming up with at least one idea that fits in each of the styles we have covered in this chapter. You might find a great idea that is hiding right behind a bad one. A brilliant name can be inspired by a stupid one. In a competitive world where every English and

Latin word has already been registered as a domain; it takes real ingenuity to come up with ideas that strategically and functionally work. Using these style types for inspiration, you might surprise yourself with a winner.

Chapter Five
Naming Process Overview

While it is certainly true that some great brand names have been hatched over a beer, the truth is that getting a workable name usually requires a deliberate process, whether you do it yourself or hire an expert name consultant. I recommend even the most budget-restricted naming project include the following five steps. The greater your resources, the more in-depth each step can be.

1. Preparatory Research

Before thinking about names, start on an informed foundation. Your name will not exist in a vacuum. Begin with looking at your own brand strategy, offer, buyers and users. How are you planning to position your brand in the market? What unique selling proposition will you offer? How is your company and product better and different? What is unique about you, above and beyond just business considerations?

Next, examine the competitive landscape and how other companies go to market. What names do they use and what clichés are common in your industry?

Lastly, do not forget to consider internal issues. Politics, interpersonal dynamics and feelings matter. Naming is an emotional exercise. Who needs to be in on the decision and what are their biases? Check to see if there are licensing issues and other legal constraints.

2. Creative Brief

Write a formal brief that spells out your findings, the implications for creating the name, and the strategic parameters that the name must serve. Provide what creative direction you can, including tastes, biases, and name types and styles to consider. It helps to provide concepts that can serve as a basis for creativity—the richer, the better. You can't hope to be different if you describe your company and your goals with the same words everyone else uses. A strong creative brief will identify ahead of time the criteria you will use to judge concepts so you can avoid falling into the "likeability" trap. The next chapter includes a list of questions that can inspire you or your naming consultant to create productively.

3. Name Generation

Creative sessions and idea exploration are the heavy lifting of the naming process. Naming consultants use dozens of techniques and resources to create a pool of ideas numbering in the hundreds. They will bring you ideas with multiple inspirations and will use a number of the name styles I discussed in Chapter Four. During this phase of work, most naming consultants do some preliminary screening, removing the obviously bad ideas, and eliminating names that don't have a clear dot-com domain (if that has been established as important in the creative brief). The top dozen or so candidates are then ready for presentation and evaluation.

4. Evaluation

Each of the top dozen name concepts should then be evaluated to the fullest degree possible, given the available resources of time, money and manpower. Kicking names around the office to see how well people like them is not an effective way to evaluate names. I can't emphasize enough how important it is to get *outside* opinions. While your name does play an internal role, it is by no means the most important role. More than anything, your brand is your face to the public. You need to start with a name that works with people outside your company.

Chapter Eight has specific advice for evaluating names and getting these outside opinions. Formal qualitative and quantitative market research into linguistics, semantics, pronunciation, visualizations, associations, and cultural relevance are common in big budget naming projects. Small companies with tiny budgets can still effectively evaluate names with a little ingenuity. Often, companies will return and conduct a second more focused round of name creation based on first round feedback.

5. Selection and Implementation

Once you have your top candidates, waste no time in grabbing the domain names. Good domain names can disappear in seconds; so don't wait for a trademark. Better to pay a few bucks for a domain you don't use than to pay for a trademark only to discover a squatter has grabbed your domain.

You will need to protect your name with a trademark. I recommend you have your lawyer apply to register your top candidate. Make sure you have at least two backups, just in case.

Once your name is protected, you will want to consider a tagline and other copy, certainly a logo and perhaps a supporting visual system.

You will need to launch the name internally to your own people and externally to customers, prospects and the public at large. Chapter Eleven contains details and advice for this phase of work.

A formal process will help you manage the job of naming your brand more effectively. While it still might be fun to come up with ideas over a couple of beers (personally, I find gin to be much more effective), a clear methodology will give you a better chance of ultimate success.

Chapter Six
The Creative Brief

A written creative brief will define success from the start. A thoughtful write-up will give you and your team a solid understanding of your strategy, the market, competitors, and implications for creating a brand. The following questions will help you on your way to a creative brief that will focus your team around objective criteria, whether you are working with a group of friends or an expert name consultant.

Differentiate Above All Else

Be sure to think in terms of what is truly different about your brand. If you use the same vague words that everyone else uses, you will end up with plain vanilla name concepts. Every company claims to provide quality. Get beyond boring and overused words and define exactly what you mean by quality. Similarly, most companies also claim to be dynamic. Exactly *how* are you dynamic? Give specific and even lengthy examples. Don't be afraid to tell a story.

Compare corporate vision and mission statements from thousands of companies and you will see the same dozen words repeated over and over. If you are tempted to talk about being customer-centric, professional, value-oriented, ethical, innovative, focused or efficient; or you claim your company displays leadership, integrity or excellence, you are saying what every company says. Remove those clichés from your creative brief. Take the time to dig down to get to what makes your brand truly special. Use evocative and meaningful words to describe that specialness.

Keep in mind that there are likely similar products with a vision similar to yours. I'm realize I am beating a dead horse here by repeating this endlessly, but being different is so important and so few people dare to do it. Check out competitive Web sites to see if all of your competitors are talking about the same blah, blah, blah. I have never met a sales organization that does not talk about relationship building and or a retailer who does not talk about value and superior customer service. Those things are important to your business, but none help you create a differentiated brand or an outstanding name. Your worst possible outcome is to look and sound just like your competitors.

The creative brief is a bit of a misnomer. When answering the questions, do *not* be brief. This is one exercise where shorter is *not* better. The more colorful detail you provide, the more you inspire creativity.

The Preliminaries:
- What resources are available for the naming project?
- Who will be on the naming team and who will make the final decision?
- What are key dates and events that can impact the schedule?
- What is your budget?

Requirements for Usage:

- Where will the name be used? On packages, in video, on signage, etc.?
- Do you need a unique domain name? What qualifiers and descriptions might be added to the name to secure a clear domain?
- What other existing elements of your business might compliment or contradict your name?
- What existing names are in use? Will your product name need to work with your corporate name?
- What legal restrictions are in place? Do partnership agreements and licenses impact decisions?

The Basic Facts:

- Describe your business, product or service in 100 words.
- Can you boil that down to one sentence?
- How about just three words?
- What are the key benefits you provide? (And one more time: avoid overused concepts such as quality, innovative, value, trust, customer-centric, efficient, professional, experienced/expert, knowledgeable; every company claims to offer these benefits.)
- How are you different from alternatives? (Again, no clichés)
- What is the single most important thing you want your brand name to convey?

Some History and Background:

- Why was this company started or product invented? What was the inspiration?
- Can you boil that down to one sentence?
- Is there anything unique, special or important about the founders or their vision and philosophy?

- Describe the place of work (geography, location, building, special features, etc.)
- Is there something special about the personality or qualities of the company or people behind it?
- What imagery comes to mind when thinking about the company or products? (Think visually.)

Your Strategy:
- How are you positioned? How do you want to be perceived relative to your competitors? What is most compelling about your company or product?
- What makes you different and special? (Better, faster, cheaper? Provide the details)
- What are the features and benefits?
- If you are looking for a product name, how will it relate to the company name?

Your Customers:
- Who is the current or expected customer?
- What is the larger or next potential market? Where will growth come from?
- Who buys, who influences and who uses? Are these all the same people? Some companies have customers who are different from consumers.
- What motivates them?
- What are their values?
- What languages are important?

Competitive Landscape:
- Who are your competitors?
- How are they positioned?
- What do they use for names?
- What are the category clichés to avoid?

Internal Issues:
- Who will be involved in the naming decision?
- What history and attitudes impact the project?
- Why were the names already created rejected? List each rejected idea and why you rejected it.

Aesthetic Considerations:
- Are there any styles of names that are particularly appealing or fitting (see Chapter Four)? Are there any that can definitely be eliminated?
- What name brands, companies and Web sites are most like this company or product in terms of style and personality?
- Describe your image two years from now? Again, try to get beyond the words everyone uses. The richer and more specific you can be in your description, the more insight you give to fuel creativity.

Sparking Name Creativity Beyond Words

Don't stop with words. Take pictures of your people, your products, your office, your customer sites. Include other visual cues. Naming consultants often create "mood boards" that are visual collages of colors, textures, images and objects that start to suggest the personality and tone of your company or product. You can do the same thing. It takes some extra time, but thinking beyond mere words is a great way to kick-start name creation.

Following is a mood board we created for that organic berry farm that ultimately inspired the Ghost Tree Farms name idea.

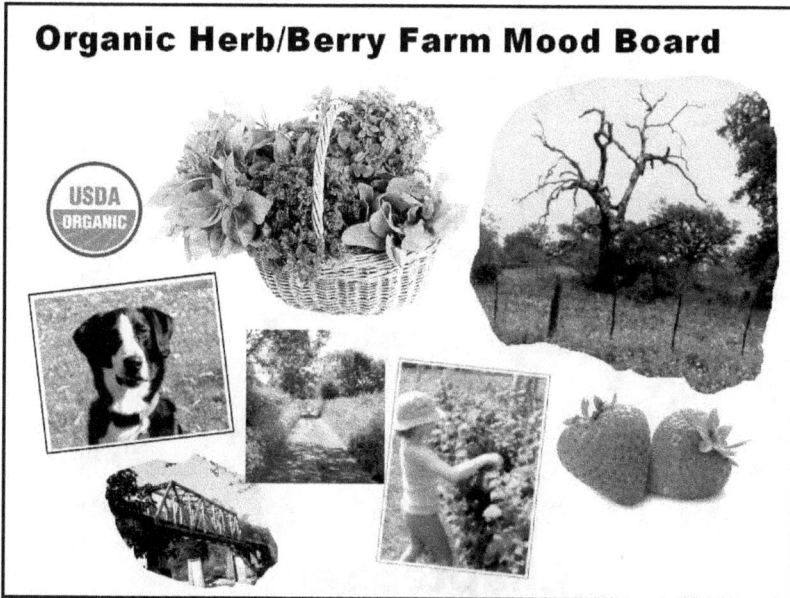

Organic Herb/Berry Farm Mood Board

The more completely and richly you are able to answer each of the questions above, the more creative you can be --either by yourself, with friends and colleagues, or working with a professional. Some of the greatest ideas come from unusual inspirations. You get the process off to the best possible start by providing as much information and insight as you can in the beginning.

Chapter Seven
Name Creation Process
and
Resources

Name creation is actually a misleading title for this chapter. Naming a company or a product is a process of *discovery* more than creation. Naming is more industry than art.

Typical creative methods like brainstorming simply don't work. Having your team sit around and come up with ideas just produces the same obvious clichés that hundreds—probably thousands—of people before you already thought of first. Thousands of new companies are created and named every day, so coming up with an unusual, distinctive, meaningful and vivid name that you can truly own is not easy. Naming is hard labor. You are going to have to dig before you find anything useful. Knowing where to dig and the tools to use will help you strike gold.

Concepting

This first step in naming does indeed have a creative aspect. The process begins with concepting—coming up with conceptual areas to explore for name ideas. Before miners start to dig for gold, they prospect. They look at the lay of the land, they sample the dirt, they sift for signs of minerals. Mining for your name begins with much the same process.

The creative brief you created in the previous chapter is your starting point. Go back to that document and go through each section, writing words and ideas that come to mind. In the Basic Facts section, examine your business description and key benefits and start listing attributes. The History and Background section may give provide inspiration around something unique about founders, vision, philosophy, work location and such. Similarly, the Strategy and Customer sections may spark your imagination. If you have taken the time to create a visual mood board, you'll find you have yet another tool for generating ideas.

When you have gone through this process, you should have a list of twenty to fifty concepts. You are ready for the next step.

Mining for Ideas

Start digging! Your prospecting for general ideas gave you a list of concepts that work as starting points. The next step is to expand on each of those concepts. When you have finished this step, you will have thousands of name ideas.

Below is a collection of some of my favorite methods and tools that can help you compile a long and inventive list.

Relate Words

Take each concept one at a time and explore related words by using a thesaurus. Online thesaurus tools make this spadework easier. Your goal is to come up with dozens of words related to each of your concepts.

http://www.thesaurus.com
I find the thesaurus from Dictionary.com to be most handy and it has a neat feature called a Visual Thesaurus that can help you jump from idea to idea.

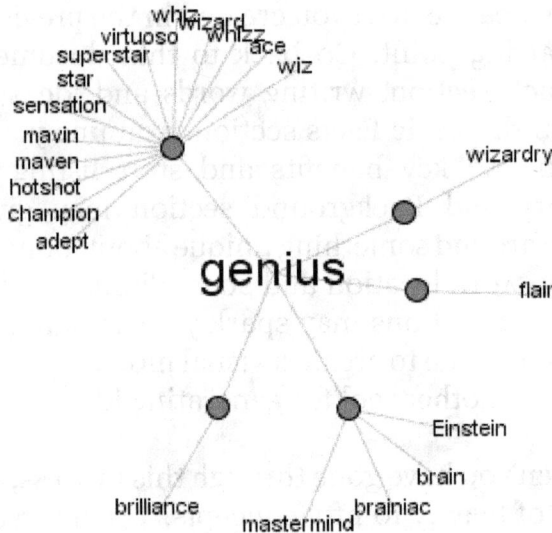

whiz wizard whizz
virtuoso ace
superstar wiz
star
sensation
mavin
maven   wizardry
hotshot
champion
adept

genius   flair

                            Einstein

                            brain
brilliance   brainiac
       mastermind

Play with Words

Now explode your twenty to fifty concepts into hundreds. You are digging out tons of ore that you will later process for gold. Start playing with ideas and create interesting variations. These sites can help"

http://www.brainyquote.com
This site is good for seeing how your word might be used

in common or clever phrases—it's how we came up with Upward Mobility for a ladder company and Punch It Up for a kickboxing gym.

http://www.aphorismsgalore.com
Aphorisms can also give you ideas for interesting phrase names. Type your concept here and you'll find lots of concepts to explore.

http://www.morewords.com
In addition to offering a great dictionary, this site is a powerful word finder. It has a feature for discovering words within other words and anagrams of words, and much more—lots of fun.

http://en.wiktionary.org
This site is invaluable for generating ideas and variations on ideas. You might find that the word you want to use doesn't have an available domain name. Come here and find etymologies, descendants, derivations, alternative forms, declensions and conjugations.

http://www.wordhippo.com
This site offers a comprehensive set of tools including a dictionary, thesaurus, rhymer, translator, phrase finder and more.

http://www.thefreedictionary.com
This is another great multi-purpose site with a number of tools, including specialized jargon dictionaries. The "idioms" section can be particularly helpful.

http://www.rhymezone.com
This site is great for finding alliterations and rhymes. One of the best features is one that allows you to find near rhymes, synonyms, homophones and more.

http://www.rhymer.com
Rhymer is another rhyming site allows you to look for beginning rhymes, end rhymes, double rhymes and more.

Foreign Words

Finding foreign words that relate to your concept is a tried and true naming method—think Acme. But don't just rush to your Latin dictionary. Try a few other languages.

http://translation.babylon.com
Babylon is fast and easy for exploring common languages.

http://www.perseus.tufts.edu/hopper/definitionlookup
This site is great for Greek, Latin, Arabic and, if you are really ambitious, Old Norse. You have the option of showing the words using Latin transliteration if you are rusty on your Greek alphabet or if you never learned Arabic characters.

http://www.stars21.com/translator
This site hosts a massive collection of online language translators—Icelandic anyone?

Name Creation

You can create names by combining parts of words (Zen plus Genius equals Zenius) or changing spelling (Physch for Fish). Here is an amazing site of linguistic resources:
http://www.utexas.edu/courses/linguistics/resources/phonetics/

You can also create words by adding a prefix of suffix. Here is an amazing collection of suffixes and prefixes, along with definitions of each one:
http://www.macroevolution.net/list-of-suffixes.html
and
http://www.macroevolution.net/list-of-prefixes.html

Stretch Your Creativity

Try generating at least five name ideas for each of the name types (*excluding* acronyms, of course) discussed in Chapter Four. This exercise forces you to think in new ways. Yes, many of the ideas won't fit or simply won't work, but digging in unexpected places may very well uncover an amazing name idea.

Play Safely

Playing with words and phrases is a great way to generate fresh ideas, but play safely. Always check your name ideas to see if they have unintended meanings. You could be surprised—possibly shocked. Look for your name in the Urban Dictionary before giving serious consideration to any idea.

http://www.urbandictionary.com

Striking Gold

If you have invested the time to do the digging, you have thousands of ideas by now. Within all that raw ore, you surely have unearthed some gold. Now you will have to sift through and refine the concepts to find the winning ideas that are unusual, distinctive, meaningful and vivid.

The next chapter shows you how.

Chapter Eight
Evaluating Names

Finding good name ideas can be tough when starting a company or creating a brand. Evaluating the ideas you create can be just as difficult. Getting hung up on all the wrong issues can turn this challenging task into an impossible one.

Stumbling Blocks to Evaluation

I have found a number of common attitudes toward evaluating names that are stumbling blocks to finding a good name:

"I'm not sure I like these ideas"

Using "likeability" as an evaluation criterion dooms your naming effort to failure. Likeability is an entirely nebulous concept that is impossible to objectively define and varies from person to person. In fact, likeability can actually be harmful as a criterion of a "good" name. Years of research have shown a strong link between likeability and familiarity.[1] People like names that are in their comfort zone of the known and conventional. That means likeable names are not going to stand out as different and they are less likely to be memorable. Being distinctive is the most important quality your name can have. A likeable name could be counterproductive. Naming is about risk taking, not risk avoidance.

"I'll know it when I see it"

Without defining your standard for a good name at the outset, you can easily find yourself frustrated when your naming team comes up with many ideas that are off the mark. Set up clear and objective name criteria in advance or you will be lost when it comes to evaluating name candidates and making a decision.

"Let's vote on our favorites"

This is where the likeability problem shows up again. Likeability is in the eye of the beholder, so you will never find an idea that everyone likes. Worse, you will end up with a name everyone can agree on, but no one loves. Chances are high that names that get the most votes will be the most likeable, the lowest common denominator, and thus will be the wrong strategic choice.

In addition to providing no usable insight for choosing a name, voting creates a negative dynamic with people who get out-voted. Voting politicizes an already emotional process.

If you are changing an existing brand or rebranding an acquired brand, you already have a political challenge. People often have strongly held biases for the old name and are not invested in what is right for the business. It will be harder to rally everyone around the strategically best name if you use the "vote-on-it" method of evaluating names.

Committees are not known to foster creativity. You are much better off having a smaller, more senior group in your organization consider all the criteria and make objective naming decisions.

"I want a name that conveys my positioning"

A single word cannot communicate a concept as complex as your company's positioning statement. Furthermore, meaning in a name is not nearly so important as the associations and connotations a word conjures. People do not puzzle over brand names; they make a snap judgment about them. A word that generates the wrong associations, regardless of its dictionary meaning, will be a disaster as a name.

A Superior Approach to Evaluating Names

With so much bad advice out there, what is the best approach for evaluating names?

Start with an understanding that the best name is the one that makes the right people (your customers) think the right things (relevant, positive, differentiating associations) about your company or product. You need to define what your brand will stand for, both in a logical sense of features and benefits, and in an emotional sense of feelings and associations. Your name has to suggest, inspire, support or reference this brand definition.

Second, you need to realize that you and the people in your company are not the best qualified people to evaluate names. Why? Because you are not the target audience for your name. To find a great name, or even a good-enough name, you have to take your concepts to your market, or at least to as many outsiders as you can.

Getting Feedback on the Cheap

Big companies spend thousands of dollars testing names with consumers. You can do research fast, cheap, and almost as well by taking your names "on tour" yourself. Taking your name candidates to potential or existing customers is ideal. Getting market-relevant feedback is invaluable. But go beyond that. Show your name candidates to regular people, too. Take them to the clerk at the dry cleaners. Ask your neighbor. Get as many reactions to your top name candidates as possible, from as broad and disconnected a group of people as you can find. It is a time consuming exercise, but you won't regret the investment. The results will almost always surprise you and you might save yourself from a disaster.

Make sure you ask for feedback the right way or you won't get useful information. Do not ask people if they *like* any of the names or even if they *understand* any of the names. Don't even tell people *what* you are naming or people will tell you if they think the name is a fit. You aren't looking for fit, meaning or likeability, but for associations and reactions. We always present name ideas to candidates this way:

> I *don't want to tell you what the names are*
> *for because I want to get your top of the*
> *mind reactions. I just want to know the **first***
> ***thought** that pops into your head.*
>
> *Please look at each idea and tell me what*
> *each name makes you think about. I don't*
> *want to know if you like the name or*
> *even if you understand the name, just the*
> ***first thing** that comes to mind, no matter*
> *what it is.*

You may need to prod people to give you the right kind of feedback. If they tell you they don't like a name, ask them to explain why. If they tell you they don't know what the name means, tell them that is okay, but that you want to hear whatever pops into their minds. Don't expect people to be linguistic experts and say, "Oh, yes, that means 'blue' in Hungarian."

I worked on a project for a company making natural and organic high end beauty and body care products. They wanted a foreign sounding name, something perhaps vaguely Asian. We created hundreds of concepts inspired by a number of different languages and having many different actual meanings, all inspired by some of the qualities of the company and its products. We took the names out to the public and asked for word associations. The resulting feedback had nothing to do with the actual meaning of the words, but we quickly found which one was the best name for the product line.

Groovy

New Age   Tranquility

Upscale   **Zenyu**   A Higher
spa   Plane

Healthy

     Enya's
Bliss   "Sail Away"

                    A car—
Town in   a Toyota   Handbags
Poland   & shoes

Sounds   Fake
kinda   **Prasada**   Prada
sad   Snooty
      McMansion   Spanish
      development Museum

People try very hard to be rational, but associations are often quite irrational. You will undoubtedly be surprised at what people have to say and they will probably apologize for their off-the-wall responses. They may not be able to articulate the reasons behind their reactions or the inspirations behind their thoughts.

Ruth Shalit, in her article for *Salon* called "The Name Game," describes an expensive West Coast naming consultant who tacked name ideas on the wall to get initial feedback from their client. One concept was the word "Jamcracker".

Several women in the group said things like "Oh, that's disgusting," and "This is really sick."

When the consultant asked them to explain what bothered them about the name, one person said, "We can't explain it, but that name is just creeping us out." The client asked that the name be taken off the wall because it bothered them so much.

The name consultant complied, but was mystified, telling Ruth, "There's apparently some strange, uncomfortable meaning attached to it in the minds of some women," he said. "God knows what that could be."

(Note--the branding company was able to sell the Jamcracker name some years after this article was published to another company that didn't have the same queasiness about it and didn't mind recycled creativity.)[2]

I recommend you get at least six people to react to each name candidate you consider. With this kind of feedback, you'll have some idea of how to tinker with your name candidates to improve reactions and associations and will know what ideas merit more exploration. The name candidates that generate rich, positive and brand-appropriate associations are the winning ideas.

Formal Research is Helpful—
If You Can Afford It

If you have money and time to invest in formal research, it is almost always worth it, particularly if your brand will need to cross cultures and languages. Large corporations commonly do qualitative research in a controlled environment with carefully selected respondent samples. I also recommend quantitative research if your budget can support it.

For global brands, you need to make sure your name does not have negative connotations in other cultures. There is an oft-repeated story of Chevrolet's Nova having a problem in Mexico because "no va" means "doesn't go" in Spanish. While the story is an urban legend, the warning is valid.[3] I once worked on a project for ExxonMobil and discovered one of our top name candidates meant "very pregnant" in Norwegian. America Online discovered their brand didn't work so well overseas--not everyone is a fan of America. Using the AOL acronym was no help. On the flip side, you can find positive connotations when your name travels. Coca-Cola means "happy mouth" in Mandarin.[4]

Expensive research is by no means required, and having it doesn't mean you won't go astray. Common sense is more useful than reams of data. US Air executives spent a fortune on hours of interviews and almost a year of analysis to discover that all they needed to do to seem like a larger, more substantial airline was to "stretch the name a little bit." That is how they made the momentous and expensive decision to make US Air into US Airways.[5] To that I say "really?"

Limitations of Feedback

While getting feedback is critical to gaining an objective perspective, don't rely on the "wisdom" of the crowd when making decisions. The opinions of others are just one input to the evaluation process. It is important to understand the limitations of outsider opinions and the common biases you will find:

- It's a drug: People have a tendency to see every new word as a drug. Unless many people make specific and consistent pharmaceutical associations and they mention nothing else, you should minimize the weight you give this particular bit of feedback.

- What does it mean? Some people will get hung up trying to decipher meaning. Unless they are linguists, it is unlikely they will guess the right definition and meaning of a name concept. They might also get hung up trying to decide what kind of product or company you are trying to name.

- Expect negativity. Many people assume you want to know what they like and don't like, no matter what you ask. It is human nature to distrust and dislike anything new, so expect negativity. You can imagine negative feedback on some successful brand names. Virgin Airlines could offend the morals of some people and suggests naiveté in an industry where expertise and sureness are prerequisite. Caterpillar is a bug responsible for destroying crops; there is nothing strong or rugged about it. And isn't Yahoo! a Swiftian fool and doesn't it sound too much like Yoohoo, the fake chocolate drink? The more provocative the name, the more negative feedback you will get—and paradoxically—the more potential it will have.

Can You Own It?

The last hurdle for evaluating names is determining if you can own the name. Owning a name has two components:
1)   Owning the trademark
2)   Owning the domain name

Think hard about the trade-offs you may have to make to get a brand name with an available domain name. Just about every English word and nearly every Latin word have already been registered as dot-com domain names. If you want a simple word like Twitter, you'll have to pay its owner dearly for it. Name candidates owned by squatters can cost anywhere from a few hundred dollars to hundreds of thousands of dollars. If you are naming your company, owning the branded domain name is more important. If you are naming a product, it is usually less so.

If your ideal domain name is taken, do not think you can get around that problem by adding an "s" to the word or adding spaces or hyphens. Settling for a dot-net or dot-biz is no better. In both cases, you are only registering a variation of a name that someone else already owns. Yes, you can legally register the variant domain name, but you can't own that place in the customers' hearts and minds. People are busy and are bombarded by so much information that they are not going to take the time to study and remember your brand. They will not grasp the nuances between BigDeal.com and BigDeals.com with an "s" to make it plural or Big-Deal.com with a dash. Settling for a variant domain just creates confusion among potential customers and always results in lost traffic going to a competitive site.

That said, you should "surround" your name by buying those variants so no one else does. See more on this subject in Chapter Nine.

Be careful how you go about checking for domain name availability. If you use a hosting provider's site to check availability, you are giving them great data about what names might be interesting and valuable. Almost all domain registrars have had their hands slapped for "front running" domain names.[6]

Domain name front running is when a registrar, such as Network Solutions, uses the fact that you researched the availability of a particular word to signal potential valuable interest in that word as a name. They then register the domain themselves. Doing so, they lock out other registrars from selling the name, and they can then either resell the name to you at a premium price or keep it to earn revenue from ads placed on the domain's landing page.

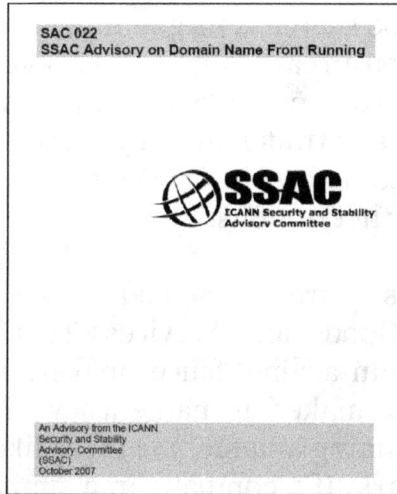

If you use any registrar's name availability search function, you risk that registrar grabbing that name. Good domains mean big money, so don't be surprised if you check one day and, lo and behold, the next day a squatter has grabbed the idea. Free WHOIS search tools (Search on "WHOIS" and "search tools" to find current versions you can load on a Windows machine—these tools are built-in on Macs) allow you to directly query the database of available domain names without broadcasting your interest in any particular word. You can also determine who is squatting a word so that you can contact them to buy it.

No matter how fantastic your name idea, if you cannot get a trademark, you'll have to discard the name. When you know what names are your top contenders, screen them for trademark availability. You can spot obvious problems with a quick search of the online trade name database called "TESS" (short for "Trademark Electronic Search Service") operated by the United States Patent & Trademark Office (www.USPTO.gov). A query to the TESS database lets you see what other companies are using your name candidates and names like it.

While a TESS search is no guarantee you will get your name, it can give you an early warning of a potential problem. If no one is using your name, you will probably be able to register that name as a trademark. If you see that dozens--or hundreds--of similar names have been registered, you might want to consider other options.

Trademarks are assigned by International Classification of Goods and Services. That is how Delta is a trademark of an airline, faucet maker, dental services company, and tool maker, to name a few. Still, the fewer the companies claiming a name, the more likely you will be granted a trademark. If a company in a similar business in your same goods and services class has trademarked your name or one like it, you may be shut out.

Again, a TESS search does not guarantee you will get your name, but you can get a good idea of how risky your application will be. I strongly advise you consult with an attorney who specializes in trademark law. This isn't an area to cut corners.

The Ultimate Choice

Your best name candidate is the name that most closely fits your strategic aspirations. You will have to combine the objective data you gathered from the research with your subjective gut instincts.

- Does the inspiration behind the name fit?

- Are the associations relevant and positive?

- Is the personality of the name appropriate?

- Does it sound right?

- Does it look right?

- How does it measure up against the criteria of strong names outlined back in Chapter Two?
  - Unusual
  - Distinctive
  - Meaningful
  - Vivid
  - Ownable

Naming a product or company is not easy. It is not like naming a child. Choosing a brand name is about strategic communication, not aesthetics. A rational process, driven by objective criteria, will help you identify the name that achieves your communication goals. And, who knows? With time, you may even come to "love" it.

Chapter Nine
Renaming

Naming a company is a relatively straightforward endeavor. Renaming an existing company or product is both more difficult and more risky.

Companies rebrand for a variety of reasons; some strategically valid, others not.

Growth

Does your company's brand name have the stature to grow? A name that worked for a small local company may not be able to compete on a bigger scale. Does your name make your company or product seem too mom-and-pop? Is your name tied to a specific geographic area that won't work as you add new markets? The right new name can add tremendous value to a company in terms of growing market share or in the case of an acquisition. My client SuperServer had a nice enough name for a local outsourced computing service, but it was not adequate for a company with national ambitions in cloud services. Renamed Proxios.[1] The company is growing fast.

Consistency

Presenting one single strong brand image to the world is less complex and confusing than maintaining multiple, similar brands. McCormick purchased the Schilling company in 1946 and maintained both brands for decades. Increased competition, additional acquisitions, a more mobile consumer base and international expansion made maintaining McCormick for the East Coast and Schilling on the West Coast impractical. The company rebranded their entire line under the McCormick name in 2002.[2]

New Markets, New Audiences

If your company enters a new market or introduces a new product, it may conflict with your current brand image. You may need to rebrand. When several media buying agencies owned by Interpublic partnered to create a hyper-local media analysis and planning service, none of the existing brands fit. My company was hired to rebrand the partnership as Geomentum.[3]

Relevance

As tastes change, brand names sometimes need to change, too. Kellogg's Sugar Pops responded to consumer aversion to sugary cereals by becoming Kellogg's Corn

Pops—now only "with a touch of sweetness." Kentucky Fried Chicken has de-emphasized the concept of "fried" and now goes by "KFC."

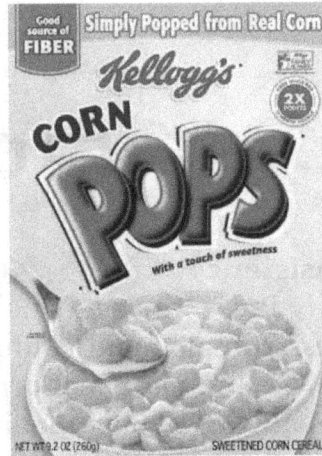

Trademark Issues

Products often need to be rebranded when a brand license expires or they run into trademark problems. Livescribe was forced to rename its Sky smartpen when News Corporation claimed the company was infringing on its BSkyB trademark.[4] Lenovo bought the temporary rights to the IBM brand name when it bought the Personal Computing Division in 2005, but had to transition to the Lenovo brand by 2010.[5]

Avoiding Negative Publicity

Companies sometimes try to run from their past. After the financial collapse of AIG in 2008, the company rebranded as AIU. The name never stuck, and, as the stink of credit default swaps dissipated, the company reverted to using the AIG name.[6] When Arthur Andersen found itself entangled in the Enron debacle, its consulting arm rebranded itself as Accenture.[7]

Mergers and Acquisitions

When two companies combine, one, the other, or both usually need to rename. Read more about M&A naming challenges in Chapter Ten.

First Do No Harm

Before considering a name change, it pays to keep in mind the key issues. In 2011, Overstock.com made a big brand blunder when the company attempted to become O.co.[8] The company failed to think through the implications. The reasons that name change failed were:

- There was never a strategic reason to change the company name. Name changes are expensive and risky in the best of circumstances. You should do it only when the benefits outweigh the costs.

- They totally owned the word "Overstock." They could never hope to own a single letter.

- The word "Overstock" worked for search engine optimization. When customers put just "o" in a search engine; the Web site didn't even show up in the top ten pages of results.

- It's tough enough to change a company's name and domain. It's even tougher when moving from the ubiquitous .com to a non-standard .co. Many non-technical people might not have even known a .co name was possible.

- The change was never tested with consumers. It is important to remember that your consumer is the ultimate "owner" of your brand. Trying to impose a change of this magnitude without even a little bit of testing with external audiences was ill-advised. O.co is what people called the company internally, but consumers did not.

Renaming Considerations

If customers don't buy into the new name or the reason behind the change, the result can be a costly disaster. The value of any name is determined by:

- Time in market: The longer a name has been used, the greater its value and the higher the risk in making a change.

- Money invested to build the brand: Making a name into a brand that people know and respect takes money. Changing it can cost as least as much. Will it be worth it?

- Extent of use: Changing a name that is emblazoned on everything from planes and trucks to uniforms and business cards, is a huge undertaking. When United Parcel Service became UPS, the job was monumentally large. Is your company up to the task?

- Customer adoption: Your brand really is the name your customers use. Federal Express bowed to consumer habits when it became FedEx. JCPenney is still JCPenney in the minds of consumers, even though it inexplicably changed its brand to JCP. You can't force your consumers to change.

- Search considerations: If your company or product depends on search engines, use great care in considering a name change. Plan for a transition and make sure the new name will help you rank near the top.

Chapter Ten
Naming Mergers and Acquisitions

Naming merged companies is a special challenge. Unlike naming a start-up or a new product, merger naming is a high stakes decision. What you ultimately decide can affect share price, the ability to integrate operations, and future growth and profitability.

Too often, names become bartering chips in merger negotiations. Letting lawyers make name decisions ignores the critical role that names play in marketing. Name decisions are *brand* decisions. Name choices should be made by carefully weighing the pros and cons of your strategic marketing options, not by legal horse-trading.

If you are lucky and the lawyers have not negotiated away your choices in naming your merger or acquisition, you have the chance to make a meaningful decision. You can select one of three naming strategies, each with its own benefits and risks.

Retain One Corporate Name

After the merger, one name survives and the other either retires or gets demoted to a divisional name or a product name. This approach provides continuity in the marketplace. One name, the strongest, most well-known, with the best chances of future growth, continues on. Because you are only rebranding one company, it is less expensive than rebranding both. On the downside, the political fall-out from these kinds of decisions can be challenging—especially if the acquiring company has to swallow its pride and take on the name of the company being bought. Employees attached to the retiring brand can feel like disenfranchised second-class citizens. You risk losing the equity of the terminated name.

This approach worked well when Mars and Wrigley merged. The merged company name remained unchanged as Mars. The Wrigley name lives on and continues to provide value to the confection and gum product line.[1]

MARS

+

= MARS

WRIGLEY

Create a Combination Name

Some companies keep both names of the merging entities as a way to keep the value of both brands alive.

By keeping both names in combination, companies try to convey the bigger brand promise of the merger. Such good intentions don't always work out. Combining names creates long, cumbersome identities and can create confusion in the marketplace. The two pieces remain separate, though together, which complicates merger politics and impedes integration. Because both parties in the merger need to rebrand, it can be just as costly as a completely new name.

Some companies use a combination name for a short period of time as a transition in rebranding. British Petroleum and Amoco went to market as BPAmoco from their merger in 1998 until they rebranded the entire entity as BP in 2000.[2]

I worked with Exxon and Mobil after they merged in 1999. They continue to successfully use their combined name today. ExxonMobil is the corporate name and the heritage brands, Exxon and Mobil separately focus on different customer segments at the product level to appeal to a broad spectrum of the market.[3]

EXXON

+   = ExxonMobil

Mobil

Create a New Corporate Name
Companies can make a clear statement of change (both internally and externally) by adopting a totally new name. A new name gives you the opportunity to establish a new identity and redefine your value proposition. Choosing

this option means you will lose the equity of the both heritage brands when you discard them for the new name. You can mitigate this risk by demoting the former company names to division or product names. In either case, the cost can be considerable.

When Bell Atlantic acquired GTE, neither brand was particularly well loved. The merged company took the opportunity to restart with a new name and they had the marketing budget to make it work.[4]

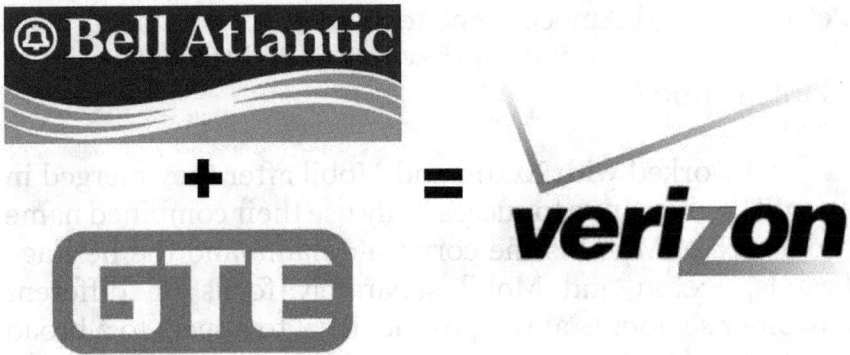

The combination of two icons of the road, however, has been much less successful. Both Roadway and Yellow were extremely strong and well-known trucking brands. Both names were retired and replaced by the non-entity of YRC (I have to just say again: no initials EVER!). Executives claim that the initials express the combined strength of both companies.[5] But the reality is the initials mean nothing. It is hard to imagine YRC ever achieving the stature of either of the two names left behind. Said one union member, "Yellow was a brand name. Roadway was a brand name. Now they come up with YRC? The YRC name is MUDD. They messed up this whole thing."[6]

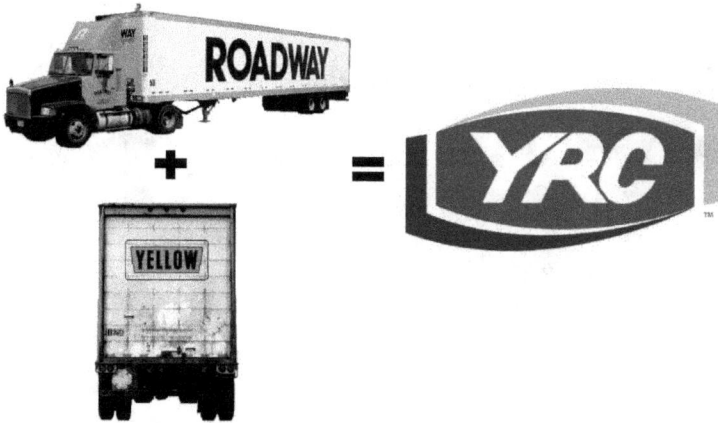

Making the right decision about which re-naming approach to adopt depends on:

* The positioning and image of the existing names: How closely are they aligned in meaning and appeal to market segments?

* The value of the existing names: How much do they contribute to profit margins, volume growth, and customer loyalty?

* Flexibility of each name: Can either or both names stand for a different or bigger value proposition?

* Geographic scope: How far does each name stretch geographically?

In the final analysis, the aspirations of the new company, the willingness of management to take risks, and the resources available to invest in naming, will drive--or at least impact—the naming decision you ultimately make.

Chapter Eleven
Implementing Names

Now that you have a name, you have taken the first step in creating a brand. Yet even the greatest name will never be a great brand without solid execution. This chapter outlines the next steps to take in building your brand.

Grab Your Domain and Then Some

Waste no time in staking a claim to the name you choose. Naming is incredibly competitive. Good ideas can be snatched away in hours. Before you do anything, do what you can as *fast* as you can to establish ownership of your name and take up as much "space" around it as possible.

Buy the domain name immediately—even before you are sure you will use the name. In most cases, getting a clear domain name is extremely important. It is better to spend a few dollars on a domain you don't need than to risk losing a great domain by debating and waiting.

Buy your brand name dotcom domain name, but do not stop there. Buy every conceivable variation of your name. This practice is called "surrounding" your brand and pays off handsomely in increased traffic and reduced brand infringement. If your brand is "Pet Source", buy "Pet-Source" and "Pets-Source." Buy the .org, .net, and .biz. Buy misspellings, too. You will increase the chances you get all the traffic due you. It doesn't hurt to block out negative names like "PetsSourceSucks" or "HatePetsSource" either.

Keep competitors from getting a domain anywhere close to your brand name. The people who bought DeltaCorp.com allowed another company to chip off a piece of their brand, confuse customers, and steal their traffic when they failed to also register the domains of Delta-Corp.com, Delta_Corp.com, DeltaCorp.net and even DeltaCorporation.com.

While you are at it, buy up tag lines and key phrases. Think of what words your customers might use to search for the service or product your company provides. Register as many of those words and phrases as domain names as you can. Owning those domains may not guarantee you top placement within search engine results, but every little bit helps. At the very least, you block your competitors from registering those domains, and you create a big footprint for your brand online.

By grabbing the most "space" around your name online, you make sure no one takes a domain that is too similar to yours or runs a site that siphons your traffic and confuses your customers.

Stake Your Trademark Claim

Get your lawyer started on the trademark process right away. Even though you ran a TESS search and are confident that you will secure a trademark on your first choice, provide your attorney with at least two back-up names. You will save time and expense should your first choice fall through.

You also need to eventually trademark your logo. Do not hold up registering your name trademark while you wait for the design of your visual brand. Someone else might grab your name in the interim. If you wait for your logo before registering your name, you could invest in a great design only to discover your name can't be trademarked after all. It is better to trademark your name first, then return later when you have a logo to amend your filing.

Complete Your Identity

Your logo is the graphic representation of your brand. You can take several different approaches to logo design:

The Typographic Mark: This kind of logo is the most common choice—39% of the top 100 global brands have typographic marks.[1] They use distinctive lettering of the name as the logo.

Typograhic marks are flexible in both a design sense and a business sense. Design flexibility means your logo doesn't compete against other graphic elements in brochures, packaging, Web pages, etc. Business flexibility means it can evolve to work with new products and sub-brands. Typographic marks cost less to implement.

The Symbol: On the other end of the spectrum are logos that are just a symbol—no words necessary. Symbolic logos transcend language and create an iconic presence for your brand. Only 3% of the top brands in the world are strictly symbol brands.[2] Such marks require time, an enormous budget, and wide distribution to become well known enough to have meaning without the presence of the brand name. Very few brands can succeed with "the artist formerly known as Prince" approach.

The Combination Mark: To get the best of both worlds, some designers use both a word mark and a symbol together.

Having both a symbol and a name gives people two cues to memory. The symbol can add meaning and can communicate a message that supports the name. If the name is not particularly unique, adding a symbol can make it easier to trademark. All too often, companies just add a random symbol to their names. These symbols have no particular relevance or meaning and use visual clichés, like the ubiquitous swoosh and globe. If you can't think of anything visual to add to the typography, don't add anything at all. The designers of the BlackBerry logo surely have an explanation of what the logo means, but do those blips next to the BlackBerry name mean anything to the average person? Even big brands with huge budgets sometimes cop out with pointless blobs next to their names. Don't make the same mistake and waste an opportunity do something with real impact and distinctive meaning.

The Emblem: Some companies make their name intrinsic to their symbol. The logo becomes a compact, self-contained expression, with the design and the name forming one entity. The logo acts as a badge or stamp and is particularly useful for consumer products.

This approach works best for short names. While an emblem can be inflexible from a design point of view, people are less prone to misusing the mark. They can't detach the name from the symbol or reorient the design, such as moving the symbol from front to back or from above to below, or removing it altogether. The self-contained nature of emblem logos makes keeping the mark's integrity easier.

Beyond the Logo

The most basic elements of brand identity are a name and a logo. However, these two elements alone are too superficial to communicate a rich brand story. Your own personal identity is more than your name and your face. It includes your personal style, your clothes and such data as your birthday, place of residence, where you work, and your phone number. It also includes the sound of your laugh, the way you walk, and the taste of your most famous recipe.

As your own personal identity is multidimensional, so should be the identity of your brand. Think beyond name and logo to how you can appeal to the five senses. Can your logo move and animate? What colors, shapes, symbols, textures, sounds, vocabulary, smells, flavors, and styles can be associated with your brand? As more customers experience your brand in an interactive environment, adding more dimensionality to your brand will help you stand out and engage. Creating a rich brand identity more effectively communicates what makes your brand so special, compelling and worth remembering.

Verbal Trademark	Visual Trademark	Trademark Sound
"Can you hear me now?"		 NBC

Trademark shapes and forms	Olfactory trademark	Trademark flavor

Telling Your Brand Story with Words

Your name is a good start on the verbal side of branding. To convey the fuller story, you need more than just one word. Brand copy includes everything from tag lines to hundred-page Web sites.

Tag lines: Call it a tag line, strapline, or slogan, many brands benefit from adding a succinct, catchy tag line to their brands. Just like names and logos, tag lines can take a number of forms:

- **Descriptive**—BMW takes a straightforward approach with the line "The Ultimate Driving Machine," while Rice Krispies describes the experience with "Snap! Krackle! Pop!"

- **Benefit Based**—Disney's promise is to be "The Happiest Place on Earth" and FedEx delivers "The World on Time."

- **Point of Difference**—John Deere states "Nothing Runs Like a Deere," 7-Up is "The Uncola," pork is "The Other White Meat" and Bounty is "The Quicker Picker Upper."

- **Witty Catchphrase**—Budweiser had "Wassup" and the California Milk Processor Board asks "Got Milk?"

- **Personality**—"Pardon Me, Do You Have Any Grey Poupon?" contrasts with Hooters "Delightfully Tacky, Yet Unrefined."

- **Visionary**—GE is "Imagination at Work" and DuPont is about "The Miracles of Science."

- **Provocative and Motivating**—AFLAC suggests "Ask about It at Work" and Michelin reminds us "Because So Much Is Riding on Your Tires."

Copy Components: You will need longer blocks of copy, too. I recommend making a list of components you need and having them professionally written. These same blocks can be re-used across various media. Having a kit of professionally written copy blocks saves people from having to constantly rewrite the same material—often with wide variations in quality and meaning. Repetition is good, so use and reuse the same components everywhere. People need multiple exposures to your story before they remember, understand and believe it. Commonly used blocks include:

- Company Description that describes who you are, what you do and the value you provide

- Boilerplate that functions as the blurb commonly used at the bottom of press releases and in catalog entries

- Unique Selling Proposition is a single, succinct sentence that encapsulates your value and key difference to the market

- Mission, Values and Vision statements are also useful

- Proof Points describe how you deliver value

- Features & Benefits provide detail for each of your claims

- Product Descriptions are needed for each product and service your company offers

- An "About Us" blurb is useful for brochures and Web sites

- History tells of your company's founding, background and achievements

Every company will have unique needs for copy blocks. Many companies compile copy blocks into a writing guide that includes information about brand vocabulary, tone, personality, key words and phrases.

Visual System

Taking a systematic approach to the way you present your brand visually, whether on your Web site, in brochures, business cards, and even videos, will dramatically strengthen the power of your brand. At the same time, you can cut your production budget. You won't have to reinvent the wheel every time you go to design something.

Creating a tool kit of graphics, typography, color palette, and imagery will turbo-charge the visual impact of your communications. Instead of each piece standing alone, they work together, build on each other, and create a unified and consistent brand across media, products, audiences, cultures, functions, and parts of your organization. You will save money in the long run because you won't have to start from scratch every time you want to design a piece of communication.

Coca-Cola, for example, uses a typographic style for the brand signature that you can recognize no matter what the language.

The brand is also easily recognized by other graphic elements including the proprietary Coca-Cola red color, the dynamic ribbon, and the fizzy bubbles.

The brand's visual style is carried out in trademarked bottle and glass shapes, characters, and more.

Launching the Name and Spreading the Word

As the saying goes, you only have one chance to make a good first impression. That is why adopting a new name isn't just an exercise in creativity. It takes some heavy duty planning. Though you may be eager to tell everyone about your new name, make sure you have all the pieces in place before you do. Interest in your company or product will be heightened when you launch a new brand name, both with the public and with your own people. Do it right, and you'll create an image of competence and maximize the opportunity to get your message out. Do it wrong, and you waste that opportunity—or worse—look slap-dash and disorganized.

You can make a strong first impression with these steps in mind:

Plan Ahead: Work with your team to identify every place the new name will be used. Find out what materials need to be created and what things need changing. Figure in lead times and dependencies for every task. Some things will be easy, like ordering business cards. Others could take weeks, like designing a Web site or replacing the sign out front.

Consider all the details like redesigning contracts, order forms and invoices, and painting trucks. Work with human resources, operations, information technology and other functional areas that will be impacted by the new name. Don't set a launch date until you know what you need and when all the pieces will be ready.

Educate the Communicators: You should take time to train the people in your organization who will be most involved in using the brand. These people include your marketing and sales departments, marketing agencies (ad agencies, PR agencies, interactive agencies, promotional agencies, etc.), distributors and other partner organizations, customer service reps and the like.

Launch Internally: You need to make sure all of your employees are on board before you make the new name public. Don't worry too much about "leaks." Better that than having your staff find out in the news or from a surprised customer. A formal internal launch is a good time to bring everyone together to celebrate. Many companies hand out a commemorative brand booklet that discusses the new name and brand, the thinking behind it, and the vision for moving forward. A gift item and a set of new business cards are a good idea, too. In a name change scenario, you may wish to have a ceremonial cleaning out of the old materials as part of the internal launch. Your corporate leaders should host the internal launch event and give the staff some idea of the change process and schedule. Internal launches are usually a week to several days before the public announcement. For a very complex company, a month or more of lead-time is not unheard of.

Public Launch: When your Web site is ready to go live, your brochures are printed, and your staff is armed with new business cards, you are ready to unveil your new name to the public. We recommend launching in two phases. A day or two before you issue the press release, you may wish to give your key customers advance notice. The new name announcement gives you an opportunity to reinforce the value you are providing to them and to brief them on your vision for the future. A letter with a brochure and a gift item are an effective approach. For your largest clients, a call from the CEO or even an insiders' lunch can be extremely effective. Work with your agencies to make the most of your public announcement. At the very least, you will need to issue a press release. Some companies stage events and unveilings as well. Make sure that you make the new name, logo, and key messaging easily accessible on your site—don't require people to register for credentials and a password. The introduction of a new brand creates an instant news angle and you want to be sure to make the most of it.

Chapter Twelve
Name Architecture

Most companies have just one brand name. Yet others own dozens or even hundreds of names as they grow and add products and services through innovation or acquisition. It does not take long before you have a name portfolio problem on your hands. Some naming consultants call this subject brand architecture. You have a name portfolio problem if you are wrestling with questions such as:

- Should you use your company name for everything you sell or does every product need a name of its own?

- What kinds of names should you adopt? What should drive the choices?

- Should you use your company name with your product names or just the product name alone?

- Does the corporate name add or subtract value to division names or product names?

- If you do not attach the company name to the product name, will people appreciate the breadth of your company?

- Do you have true brands that are delivering value to your company or do you have a collection of names that no one outside the company really uses or remembers?

- What if your product names outshine the corporate name? Think RIM vs. BlackBerry.

- What are the pros and cons of the ad hoc status quo? What are potential future impacts if you don't deal with the problem strategically?

- Can your current name take you into new markets and new businesses?

- What do you do with all the brand names you get with each acquisition? With some of your products overlapping, how do you know which names to eliminate?

Taking the right approach to naming your products and services will build value, reduce market confusion, trim waste, and prevent missed opportunities. Improving your name strategy can improve business performance and support your business strategy.

Business Strategy

Name Strategy

Four Approaches to Naming Architecture

You have a number of options in deciding how to structure the brand names in your portfolio:

One Name for Everything

One name covers everything your company sells. Divisions and products are denoted by a clear description. The "one name" approach makes marketing more efficient. With one name front and center, cross-selling and cooperation are easier. On the downside, the brand can lose focus, as the name must be everything to everybody. Acquired companies might be reluctant to have their heritage brand names disappear. New businesses might not fit under an inelastic single brand.

Multiple Names

Decentralized companies that target diverse markets favor a multiple name structure. Each brand focuses on a specific market target. Brand names function as independent entities and can even compete against other names within the portfolio. While acquiring and divesting companies is relatively simple, investors do not always recognize the scope and value of the company as a whole. Supporting many names is expensive and time consuming. Cross-selling and cooperation are more difficult.

The WALT DISNEY Company

Hybrid Approach

Market pressures, organizational dynamics and limited budgets often make a hybrid approach more realistic. Companies use hybrid name structures with varying degrees of flexibility. The corporate name endorses the product or service name like the Marriott name endorses Courtyard.

Endorsing Brand

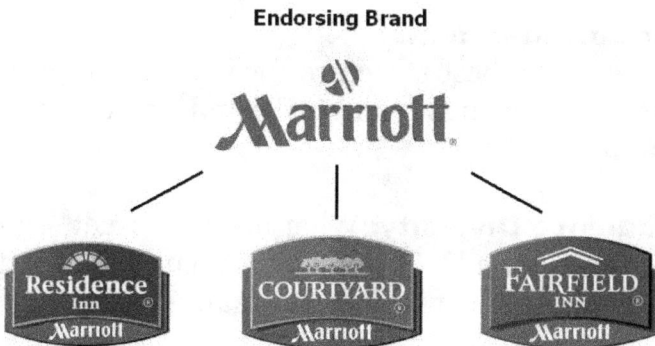

Alternatively, the product or service name can function as a sub-brand of the corporate name like the Silverlight name is a sub-brand of Microsoft.

Sub-Brands

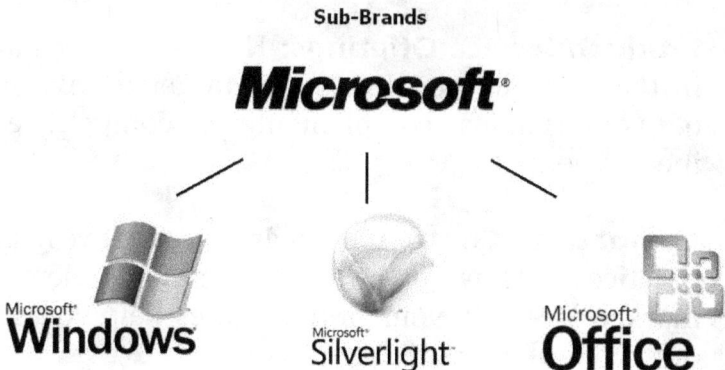

Mixed Approach

Most companies use more than one approach. GE is known for its "one name" approach, but it has exceptions. The NBC brand is separate and unassociated with the GE brand.

Strategic Considerations

What is the best structure for your name portfolio? The answer depends on a number of strategic considerations.

- **Audience Diversity:** What are the target segments for your brand? Is the name focused on just one audience or must it appeal to many?

- **Brand Elasticity:** How far can each of the names stretch to cover different products and markets? Harley Davidson made a classic blunder applying their name to wine coolers.

- **Product/Service Offerings:** How are other names in the portfolio positioned and targeted? Are some of your names complementary, competitive or incongruent?

- **Competitive Context:** What are competitive naming practices? How do your customers view the marketplace? Do your brand names help you stand out and grab market share?

- **Brand Equities:** Do you have names with a particular following or a unique heritage and equity that must be carried forward?

- **Geographic Needs:** How consistent are needs or preferences across cultures and markets? Strong local names might not work in other countries. Not every name can "travel."

- **Organizational Structures:** Who is accountable for naming practices and standards? What licensing agreements are in place? What are the political realities behind names in your portfolio?

- **Ownership:** Does the organization have legal control over its brand name? You'll have less leeway with licensed names.

- **Sources of Growth:** What businesses and products are expected to drive future growth for your company? Are their names helping you pursue your strategy?

- **Purchase Criteria:** How do people buy your products? Do they ask for products by brand name, company name, or a generic name? Do your names make buying easier or do they add a layer of confusion?

- **Brand Role:** What role does your brand name play in fulfilling your business model? How important is the brand name in driving awareness or creating loyalty?

- **Channels:** What channels and distribution methods are available? How are they used across your portfolio of brand names?

- **Company-Specific Issues:** What considerations are specific to your company or industry? Approaches that are technically most appropriate might not be feasible in the reality of your company. Things like politics, legal structures, and partner demands muddle theoretical purity. Sometimes theory has to bow to practicality.

Company culture, goals, markets and customers will drive the right name structure for your company. You can save yourself and your company both trouble and expense by thinking about a naming strategy early, before problems have time to take root.

Chapter Thirteen
Making a Worthy Name

Naming your company or product is an important first step in creating a brand. While it isn't easy, naming doesn't have to be a long, arduous process that costs an arm and a leg. The important things to remember are:

1. **Follow a process**

   You don't have to spend months in analysis and testing, but you will definitely benefit from having a process than having a few friends come up with some ideas over a beer (or a martini).

2. **Dig deep**

   Explore what makes your company or product different. Look at what drives personality. Go beyond the superficial things and literal meanings. Creativity is worth the risk.

3. **Don't do boring**

Reset the standards for your industry. Take a leap. Don't think teeth and smiles if you are a dentist. Move beyond thinking about homes if you are a real estate agent. Don't pick the name that everyone can agree on, but that no one gets excited about.

4. **What you like doesn't matter**

What matters most is what your customers think. Your own biases are of little consequence. You might fall in love with a word that literally means "worth trusting", but if your customers think the word means "metrosexual deodorant", it is a bad choice. Always seek associations and connotations from people outside your organization. Then heed what they have to say.

5. **Look at the big picture**

The name is just the start. Think how it will work as a logo, within a visual system, on products and out in the world.

No doubt, naming has gotten tougher as our world has grown more connected and communication has taken so many new forms. Those same forces also make your name more important. The days when you could call your company American Telephone & Telegraph Company are long over. With smart choices and savvy marketing, you can build a brand worthy of your name.

Notes

Chapter One The Role of Name in Branding

1. Christopher Boyce, "New logo is just ducky for marketing Columbus, Ga.-based insurer Aflac," *Columbus Ledger-Enquirer* (Columbus, GA, December 3, 2004).

2. Dr. E.L. Kersten, Despair, Inc. Press Release (Santa Clara, CA - June 29, 1999).

Chapter Two Naming Criteria: What Makes a Good Name

1. Ann Byers, *Jeff Bezos: The Founder of Amazon.com*, The Rosen Publishing Group: 2006, pages 46-47.

2. U.S. Patent & Trademark Office TESS search on word "Delta". Conducted October, 29, 2009.

Chapter Three Domain Name Hang-Ups and Watch-Outs

1. Alexandra Biesada "Walgreen Co." *Hoovers, Inc.*, www.hoovers.com. Retrieved October 29, 2009.

2, Rachel Pierce, "Drugstore.com, Inc." *Hoovers, Inc.*, www.hoovers.com. Retrieved October 29, 2009.

3. "Top 50 Drug Chains," *Chain Drug Review*, October 27, 2008.

Chapter Four Ideas to Consider Types of Successful Names

1. "History", CVS Caremark Corporation, http://info. CVSCaremark.com/our-company/history. Retrieved October 29, 2009.

2. Alexandra Biesada "QVC, Inc." *Hoovers, Inc.*, www. hoovers.com. Retrieved October 29, 2009.

3. "T.G.I.Friday's History," *T.G.I. Friday's Inc.*, http://fridays.mediaroom.com/index.php?s=64. Retrieved October 29, 2009.

4. "Mr. Scott McNealy," *Sun Microsystems, Inc.*, 2005-04-24. http://www.sun.com/products-n-solutions/ edu/gelc/bios/scottmcnealy.html. Retrieved 2009-09-17.

5. Maxine Laurie and Marc Mappen, *Encyclopedia of New Jersey*, p. 555 (Rutgers University Press, 2004/2005).

6. "History", *7-Eleven, Inc.*, http://www.7-eleven.com/ AboutUs/History/tabid/75/Default.aspx. Retrieved October 29, 2009.

7. "FAQs: V8© 100% Vegetable Juice" *CSC Brands LP*, http://www.v8juice.com/FAQ.aspx. Retrieved October 29, 2009.

8. "Our Company" *Qantas Airways Limited*, http:// www.qantas.com.au/travel/airlines/company/ global/en. Retrieved October 29, 2009.

9. "NTT DoCoMo: Review of a Case," *Japan Media Review,* http://www.ojr.org/japan/research/ 1097446811.php. Retrieved October 29, 2009.

10.   "Gazprom Nigeria venture, Nigaz, stirs racism debate," *Reuters Africa,*Wed Jul 1, 2009.

11.   Robert Pripps, *The Big Book of Caterpillar* (Voyageur Press, MN, February 2000) page 32.

12.   "Apple Facts," *The Apple Museum,* http://www. theapplemuseum.com/index.php?id=44. Retrieved October 29, 2009.

13.   "Reebok History," *Reebok International Limited,* http://corporate.reebok.com/en/reebok_history/ default.asp#1950-1980. Retrieved October 29, 2009.

14.   Gary Rivlin, "A Retail Revolution Turns 10," *New York Times*, July 10, 2005.

15.   Terry Edwards, "The Story of Altoids," *Associated Content,* September 27, 2006.

16.   Jonathan P. Hicks, "Firestone to Sell 75% of Tire Unit In $1 Billion Deal With Japanese,"*New York Times*, February 17, 1988.

17.   "Origin of the Logo", *Canon, Inc.,* http://www. canon.com/about/mark/origin.html. Retrieved October 29, 2009.

18.   "The history of the Volvo brand name," *Volvo Owners Club*, http://www.volvoclub.org.uk/history/ brand-history.shtml. Retrieved October 29, 2009.

19.   "Hitler's car for the people: Known and unknown sides of the experiment," *Guardian Century,* 5 January 1939, http://century.guardian. co.uk/1930-1939/Story/0,,127261,00.html.

20. "Samsung Manufacturing Information", *Top Ten Reviews*, http://tv.toptenreviews.com/flat-panel/lcd/samsung-manufacturing-information.htm. Retrieved October 29, 2009.

21. "Toyota Traditions," *Toyota Motor Corporation*, http://www2.toyota.co.jp/en/vision/traditions/nov_dec_04.html. Retrieved October 29, 2009.

22. Wolfgang Saxon,"Marcel Bich, 79, Dies; Cheap Pens Yielded Riches," *New York Times*, June 1, 1994.

23. "Man who gave name to Danone dies aged 103," *Reuters*, May 18, 2009.

24. "About Adidas: Adi Dassler - the man who gave adidas its name," *Adidas*, http://www.press.adidas.com/DesktopDefault.aspx/tabid-28/41_read-1203/ Retrieved October 29. 2009.

25. Mark R. Wilson, Stephen R. Porter, and Janice L. Reiff, "Bally Manufacturing Corp." *Dictionary of Leading Chicago Businesses (1820-2000)* , 2005, Chicago Historical Society.

26. "The History of Arby's," *GZK Restaurant Systems, Inc.*, http://www.arbysdayton.com/history/. Retrieved October 29, 2009.

27. "Candy King Forrest Mars, Who Created M&Ms, Dies," *Seattle Post-Intelligencer*, July 3, 1999.

28. "The Chronicle Of Coca-Cola: Birth of a Refreshing Idea," *The Coca-Cola Company*, http://www.thecoca-colacompany.com/heritage/chronicle_birth_refreshing_idea.html. Retrieved October 29,

2009.

29. "The Birthplace of Pepsi-Cola," *The Pepsi Store*,
     http://www.pepsistore.com/history.asp. Retrieved
     October 29, 2009.

30. "Company History," *Dr Pepper Snapple Group,
     Inc.*, http://investor.drpeppersnapple.com/index.
     cfm?pagesect=history .Retrieved October 29, 2009.

31. Barry Newman, "No Grapes, No Nuts, No Market
     Share: A Venerable Cereal Faces Crunchtime," *The
     Wall Street Journal*, June 1, 2009.

32. "Company History," *The Clorox Company*, http://
     www.thecloroxcompany.com/company/history/
     index.html. Retrieved October 29, 2009.

33. Martin Hrobsky, "The battle over the Budweiser
     name continues..." *Radio Praha Live,* Broadcast,
     14-11-2002.

34. "Marlboro," *Encyclopædia Britannica 2009.*
     Encyclopædia Britannica Online. http://www.
     britannica.com/EBchecked/topic/365838/
     Marlboro. Retrieved October 29, 2009.

35. "Cisco Systems Corporate Timeline," *Cisco Systems,
     2008.* http://newsroom.cisco.com/dlls/corporate_
     timeline_2008.pdf.

36. Beth Blakely, "Monday: PwC Consulting's new name
     creates controversy, cackles," *Tech Republic*, Jul 17,
     2002 .

Chapter Eight Evaluating Names

1. Richard L. Moreland and Robert B. Zajonc, Exposure Effects in Person Perception: Familiarity, Similarity, and Attraction," University of Michigan, December 3, 1980.

2. Ruth Shalit, "The name game Welcome to the vicious world of corporate name-creation," *Salon*, November 11, 1999, http://www.salon.com/media/col/shal/1999/11/30/naming/print.html.

3. "Don't Go Here," *Snopes.com*, 19 February 2007, http://www.snopes.com/business/misxlate/nova.asp Retrieved October 29, 2009.

4. Tom Doctoroff, *Billions*, Palgrave Macmillan, New York 2005, page 200.

5. Ruth Shalit, "The name game: Welcome to the vicious world of corporate name-creation," *Salon*, November 11, 1999, http://www.salon.com/media/col/shal/1999/11/30/naming/print.html.

6. Enrico Schaefer, "Domain Front Running by Registrars Continues to Draw Attention," *Circle ID*, Jan 09, 2008 .

Chapter Nine Renaming

1. Frank Butler, "Rebranding for Growth: Super-Server Becomes Proxios," Richmond, VA, August 19, 2009.

2. http://www.mccormickcorporation.com/Corporate/layouts/companyHistory2000_present.aspx Retrieved March 3, 2013.

3. Steve Mcclellan, "Mediabrands Thinks 'Hyper Local' with Geomentum," *Adweek,* August 6, 2009.

4. Sharif Sakr, "Livescribe renames Sky smartpen after losing trademark dispute with BSkyB HD," *Engadget*, February 15, 2013.

5. Philip Kotler and Waldemar Pfoertsch, *B2B Brand Management,* Springer, Berlin 2006, page 255.

6. Trefis Team, "AIG Is Ready To Use Its Own Name Again For P&C Business," *Forbes,* June 13, 2012.

7. Stephen Rynkiewicz, "Andersen Consulting Accents New Name," *Chicago Tribune,* October 26, 2000.

8. Beth Snyder Bulik, "O, No! Overstock Backs Off O.co Name Change," *Advertising Age,* November 14, 2011.

Chapter Ten Naming Mergers and Aquisitions

1. Linda Rano, "Mars-Wrigley merger creates world's largest confectionery player", *Food Production Daily*, 29-Apr-2008.

2. Mitch Morrison, "BP Amoco Buys ARCO, Changes Name to BP," *Convenience Store News*, April 17, 2000.

3. Charlene Oldham, "Exxon Mobil Keeps Both Brands Alive in Effort to Retain Customer Loyalty," *The Dallas Morning News,* August 28, 2001.

4. "Corporate History," *Verizon*, http://investor.verizon.com/profile/history/. Retrieved October 29, 2009.

5.   "Rebranding for Yellow Roadway," *The Journal of Commerce Online*, January 03, 2006.

6.   "YRC to cut 1,100 jobs, close 27 terminals in regional trucking restructuring," *Topix Forum*, http://www.topix.com/forum/city/kansas-city-mo/TDE9AACGVKUOK9R7G/p2.

Chapter Eleven Implementing the Name
1.   "Top 100 Global Brands," *FT.com*, http://media.ft.com/cms/e5a01ad8-30d5-11de-bc38-00144feabdc0.pdf. Retrieved October 29, 2009.

2.   Ibid.

Index

About the Author

Lisa Merriam is a brand consultant who has made a career of helping companies build and manage brands. She has led over 200 naming projects for billion dollar Fortune 500 multinationals and tiny start-ups. Her naming experience includes business-to-business and consumer brands, in sectors as diverse as fashion, retail, technology, industrial products and more.

She is President of Merriam Associates and consults with branding, advertising and marketing agencies globally. Learn more at www.MerriamAssociates.com.

Prior to starting Merriam Associates, Lisa was a brand strategy director at McCann-Erickson's FutureBrand consultancy and was director of Marketing for E Ink, the company that innovated the technology behind Amazon's Kindle e-book reader.

Lisa is a seasoned copywriter and published author. She has written for publications such *Forbes, American Bank Marketing, Apparel Magazine, China Business News, Sporting Goods Business* and others. She has also written and illustrated a series of children's books targeted to elementary age readers. She has also been interviewed by NPR, CNN, Yahoo!, *Crain's, Success Magazine, Marketing Daily, American Express Open*, Atlanta Business Radio and others.

Lisa lives in Manhattan with her two children Lucy and Joe.

Special thanks to:

Pam Levine for her amazing eye for beauty and brand—always strategically on target. www.LevineDesignGroup.com

Milton Kotler for his deep understanding of marketing. See www.KotlerOnGrowth.com

Larry Aaron—a brilliant namer and visual branding genius. www.EverBrand.com

Amanda Strauss for style, steadfastness, patience and fun, fun, fun business. www. amandastraussdesigns.com

Randy Ringer and Michael Thibodeau at Verse Group for enlightenment and inspiration. www.VerseGroup.com

Rob McD, more than just a naming expert, a verbal design specialist, whose editing and logical challenges much improve the text. www.WordBreeder.com

The folks at Fresh Bread Creative—love working with you and *love* your agency's name. Thank you for the "daily bread." www.freshbreadcreative.com

Every former colleague at FutureBrand—thank you for teaching me my chops. www. FutureBrand.com

Patrick Roye, fellow-namer, translator and entrepreneur—boy, do I ever owe you one!

Janet Bailey for all the tedious editing—thanks Mom!

www.ingramcontent.com/pod-product-compliance
Lightning Source LLC
Chambersburg PA
CBHW072235290326
41934CB00008BA/1307